Motivational Stories for Kids

Lessons in Courage, Kindness, and the Power of Believing in Yourself

By Jesika Pagula

1. The Little Seed That Could

In a peaceful forest nestled at the edge of a mountain range, there lived a tiny seed. It wasn't the biggest or the brightest, but it had a big dream. It wanted to grow tall and strong, just like the magnificent trees that towered above it. But there was one problem: this seed was small and fragile, and the forest was full of storms, animals, and difficult weather conditions that made life challenging.

The little seed had heard stories from the older trees. They spoke of how, over many years, they had grown from tiny seeds into towering giants with leaves that reached the sky. The little seed wanted to be like them, to feel the warmth of the sun on its leaves and stretch its branches wide. It wasn't content to stay buried in the ground. The dream of reaching the sky fueled its determination.

One bright spring morning, a gentle breeze whispered through the forest. The little seed knew this was the moment. It gathered all its courage and began to push upward, determined to break free from the dark earth. The journey was not easy. The earth was heavy, and the air above seemed so far away. But the seed kept pushing, inch by inch, never giving up.

Just as the seed was beginning to break through the soil, dark clouds gathered in the sky. A mighty storm blew in, with fierce winds and heavy rain. The little seed was terrified. It had barely begun to grow, and now it was being pushed back by the wind.

Maybe it wasn't strong enough. Maybe it should just stay in the ground where it was safe.

But as the rain poured down, the seed remembered the older trees and their stories. They had faced storms just like this one and had stood tall. The seed decided to stay strong. With every gust of wind, it dug its tiny roots deeper into the soil, making itself stronger. The storm raged for hours, but eventually, the clouds cleared, and the sun returned.

The seed, though battered and weary, had not been uprooted. It had survived the storm.

Weeks passed, and the forest grew dry. The sun beat down relentlessly, and the soil began to crack. The little seed, now a tiny sprout, felt thirsty and weak. It wondered if it could survive this drought. Every day, it looked up at the older trees, whose thick branches were covered in lush leaves, and felt discouraged. They seemed to thrive while it struggled to grow.

But instead of giving up, the seed reminded itself of its dream. It wanted to grow, to reach the sky, to become part of the great forest. It decided to find a way. The little sprout stretched its tiny roots deeper into the soil, searching for moisture. It found a small stream far below the surface. With a newfound strength, the sprout absorbed the water, and though the drought continued, it managed to stay alive.

With each passing season, the little seed grew stronger. It faced more storms, more droughts, and more challenges, but with each challenge, it learned. It learned how to bend with the wind instead of breaking, how to conserve its energy during the heat, and how to reach higher for the sun. Slowly but surely, the little seed transformed into a young tree, its branches now stretching out and its roots digging deep.

The older trees noticed the young tree's determination and strength. They whispered to one another, proud of the little seed that had faced so many obstacles and still continued to grow.

Years passed, and the little seed was no longer a small sprout. It had grown into a tall, strong tree. Its branches now reached high into the sky, and its leaves rustled in the breeze. The young tree looked out over the forest, feeling the warmth of the sun and the strength of the earth beneath its roots.

One day, a young sapling approached the tree and asked how it had become so tall and strong.

The tree smiled and explained that it had once been a tiny seed, just like the sapling. It had faced many storms and many challenges, but it kept pushing forward, believing it could grow and become strong. It told the sapling that no matter how small it started, if it never gave up, it could achieve great things.

The sapling, inspired by the tree's words, promised to be strong and patient. The little seed's dream had come true. It had grown into a magnificent tree, not because it was the strongest from the beginning, but because it never gave up, no matter how hard things got.

And so, the story of the little seed that could spread across the forest, inspiring all who heard it to believe in themselves, to keep going no matter the odds, and to grow tall and strong, just like the trees.

2. The Brave Butterfly

In a quiet meadow, nestled between rolling hills and flowing streams, there was a small caterpillar named Luna. Luna was not like the other caterpillars. While the other caterpillars seemed excited to grow and change, Luna was terrified. She had heard the older butterflies talk about the great transformation that awaited her, but she wasn't sure she was ready. What if the change was too hard? What if she wasn't strong enough?

Luna had always been a small caterpillar, moving slowly from leaf to leaf. Every day, she ate leaves to grow stronger, but she couldn't shake the fear that gripped her heart. Every time she thought about the cocoon she would need to build, her stomach filled with dread. "What if it's too dark inside? What if I get stuck?" she thought.

One evening, as Luna rested on a leaf, an older butterfly named Marla fluttered by. Marla had beautiful wings that shimmered in the sunlight, and she was admired by all the creatures of the meadow. Luna looked up at her in awe, but also with a little envy.

"Marla," Luna asked softly, "how did you become so beautiful? I'm just a tiny caterpillar, and I'm afraid I'll never be able to change."

Marla landed on a nearby flower and looked at Luna with gentle eyes. "Change is never easy, Luna," she said. "But you will become something wonderful. The key is not to fear the transformation, but to trust in it. Every butterfly has to face their fears to find their wings."

Luna listened carefully, but she still wasn't sure. The idea of being wrapped up in a cocoon, unable to move, was frightening. She decided to wait a little longer before starting the transformation, hoping that maybe the fear would go away on its own. But days turned into weeks, and Luna still hadn't made up her mind.

One morning, as the sun began to rise and the meadow came alive with the sounds of chirping birds and rustling leaves, Luna felt something stirring inside her. It was a strange sensation, one she had never felt before. She had been eating leaves and growing every day, but now, it felt as if something was calling her to change, to become something new.

With a deep breath, Luna decided it was time. She began to spin her cocoon, wrapping herself carefully in silk. As she worked, she felt the familiar fear return. "What if I get stuck?" she thought again. "What if I can't do it?" But then she remembered Marla's words. "Trust in the transformation," she whispered to herself.

As Luna settled inside the cocoon, the world outside grew quiet. She was in complete darkness, and the fear returned. There was no movement, no sound, and Luna felt alone. "Why did I do this?" she thought. "What if I never change?"

Days passed, and Luna remained inside the cocoon. Time seemed to stand still. But in the stillness, something began to shift. She felt her body change, her wings forming, her legs growing stronger. She could feel the promise of something new, something beautiful waiting inside her.

One morning, Luna felt a light touch on her cocoon. It was the warmth of the sun, and it was time. She felt the cocoon begin to crack open, and with a burst of strength, she emerged. At first, Luna was weak and shaky, but then, with a deep breath, she opened her wings for the first time.

Luna's wings were delicate and soft at first, but they quickly grew strong and beautiful. They shimmered with shades of purple, blue, and gold, and as she fluttered them, she realized she could fly. The fear she had once felt was gone, replaced by the joy of freedom.

Luna took her first flight, soaring over the meadow with Marla and the other butterflies. She could see everything from above—lush green trees, colorful flowers, and wide, open skies. For the first time, Luna felt truly alive, her heart full of courage.

From that day on, Luna was no longer afraid of change. She had faced her fears and embraced the transformation. She had trusted in the process, and in the end, she became the beautiful butterfly she had always dreamed of being.

As Luna fluttered through the meadow, she saw a young caterpillar sitting on a leaf, looking unsure and afraid. Luna flew over to him and smiled. "Don't be afraid of the change," she said. "You have everything inside you to become something wonderful. Trust in the transformation, and you will find your wings."

The young caterpillar looked up at Luna, feeling inspired by her courage. He knew now that when his time came, he would face his fears and embrace the change, just as Luna had.

And so, Luna's story spread across the meadow, teaching everyone that change, though scary, is a necessary part of life, and that sometimes, we have to be brave enough to trust in the process and embrace what's to come.

3. The Mountain Climber's Promise

In a small village nestled at the foot of a towering mountain, there lived a boy named Kai. From the moment he could walk, Kai had been fascinated by the mountains. He would often sit by the village river, gazing up at the snow-capped peaks, imagining what it would be like to stand on top, looking out over the world below. The villagers often spoke of the mountain's grandeur, but also of its dangers. Many had tried to climb it and failed, returning home exhausted, hurt, or even never returning at all.

Kai's father, a seasoned mountaineer, had tried to climb the mountain many years ago. But despite his strength and skill, he had to turn back halfway up. He often told Kai stories of the mountain's challenges: the freezing winds, the steep cliffs, and the narrow paths that seemed impossible to navigate. His father's warnings, though well-meaning, only fueled Kai's desire to climb the mountain himself.

"I want to climb the mountain, Father," Kai would often say.

His father would smile gently and shake his head. "It's not just about wanting, Kai. You must be prepared. The mountain is not kind to those who rush. It teaches patience, perseverance, and strength, but only to those who earn it."

Kai understood, but his dream of reaching the summit never faded. He spent years preparing. Every day, he practiced climbing smaller hills around the village, building his strength, and learning the ways of the mountain. He read books about climbing, watched others train, and even helped the villagers carry supplies up the smaller slopes.

One day, after many years of preparation, Kai felt ready. The village was celebrating the coming of spring, and he decided that it was the perfect time to begin his climb.

He packed his backpack with food, water, and a warm jacket, and with his heart full of determination, he set off.

As he began his journey up the lower slopes of the mountain, Kai felt the excitement of the challenge before him. The first part of the climb was relatively easy, and he quickly moved past the lower rocks, feeling proud of his progress. But as he ascended higher, the path became steeper and the air colder. The wind picked up, and the once-clear sky turned cloudy. Kai's heart began to race as he realized the mountain was beginning to test him.

The first real challenge came when he reached a narrow cliff that stretched across the mountain side. The rock was jagged, and the path was barely wide enough for his feet. One wrong step, and he could slip and fall into the abyss below. Kai hesitated for a moment. His breath came out in short gasps as the cold wind bit at his skin.

But then, remembering his father's words about patience, Kai took a deep breath. He focused on the path ahead, his hands gripping the rocks tightly. Slowly but surely, he moved forward, step by careful step, until he reached the end of the cliff. His heart pounded in his chest, but he didn't let fear control him. With a sense of accomplishment, he continued climbing.

As the days passed, the climb grew more difficult. The weather turned colder, and the air became thinner. Kai's legs ached, and his muscles grew tired. He faced storms, blizzards, and even avalanches that forced him to take cover in caves. The mountain was unforgiving, but each time Kai faced an obstacle, he pushed through, using all the skills and knowledge he had acquired.

One night, after an especially fierce storm, Kai sat in a small cave, warming himself by a fire. He felt a deep weariness in his bones. He thought about turning back, but then he remembered the promise he had made to himself: he would reach the top, no matter what it took. He had come this far. He knew he couldn't give up now.

On the final leg of the climb, the path grew steeper and more treacherous. The wind howled, and the snow was deep. Every step was a struggle, but with each step, Kai's determination grew. His hands were frozen, his face numb, and his body was exhausted. But the thought of standing on top of the mountain, seeing the world from the highest point, kept him going.

Finally, after days of relentless climbing, Kai reached the summit. As he stood there, looking out over the vast landscape, he felt a wave of relief and triumph. The wind had died down, and the clouds parted, revealing a breathtaking view of the valley below, the village, and the world stretching out before him.

Kai had done it. He had climbed the mountain. He had faced every obstacle, pushed through every challenge, and never given up. The journey had been long and hard, but the reward was worth it. As he stood at the top, he felt a sense of pride that came from knowing that he had earned this moment. He had made the mountain his own.

Kai stayed at the summit for a while, taking in the beauty around him. He thought about the lessons he had learned along the way—patience, perseverance, and the importance of never giving up, even when the road ahead seemed impossible.

When he finally began his descent, he was not just a boy who had climbed a mountain. He was a person who had faced his fears, overcome challenges, and proven to himself that he was capable of achieving anything, as long as he was willing to put in the effort.

When Kai returned to the village, the people gathered around to hear about his journey. He smiled and shared the story of his climb, not with pride, but with the understanding that the mountain had taught him far more than just how to reach the top. It had taught him that the journey, with all its struggles and setbacks, was just as important as the destination.

Kai's story inspired many in the village, and over time, the villagers came to understand the true meaning of climbing the mountain: it wasn't about conquering it. It was about the lessons learned along the way, the strength found in persistence, and the growth that comes from facing challenges head-on.

4. The Kindness of the Little Fox

Deep in the heart of a vast forest, there lived a small, curious fox named Finn. Finn was known by all the animals for his bright orange fur and his playful nature. But what made Finn truly special was his big heart. He always looked for ways to help others, whether it was gathering food for the birds or helping the rabbits find shelter from the rain. Even though he was just a little fox, he believed that kindness was the most important thing in the world.

One chilly autumn morning, Finn was wandering through the forest when he noticed something strange. A large, dark cloud had appeared above the trees, and the winds had begun to howl. As he wandered deeper into the woods, he found that the storm was only growing stronger, and the trees swayed under the force of the wind. The ground became slick with rain, and the forest grew quiet as the animals hurried to find shelter.

Finn was a little scared himself, but he knew that others would need his help. He scampered quickly to a group of rabbits huddled near a large oak tree. They looked worried, their fur damp from the rain.

"What's wrong?" Finn asked, his voice full of concern.

"The storm is too strong," said one of the rabbits. "We can't find our burrow, and we're too afraid to go out in the storm."

Finn's heart sank. He couldn't let the rabbits stay out in the cold and wet. "Don't worry," he said. "I'll help you find shelter."

With that, Finn led the rabbits through the woods, his small paws quickly finding the best path through the trees. The rain lashed against them, and the wind howled, but Finn remained determined. After what felt like an eternity, they finally found a dry, safe cave beneath a large boulder. The rabbits hopped inside, grateful for the shelter.

"Thank you, Finn," one of the rabbits said, her eyes wide with gratitude. "We were so scared."

Finn smiled warmly. "I'm happy I could help," he said. "Stay here and stay dry. I'll check on the others."

As Finn made his way deeper into the forest, the storm continued to rage. He soon encountered a family of birds, their feathers soaked from the rain, perched on a branch high in a tree. They looked worried and cold, unable to fly in the storm.

Finn thought for a moment. "I'll bring you somewhere safe," he said. "Follow me closely!"

The fox dashed through the rain, his small body darting between the trees. He led the birds to a small hollow in the ground where they could rest, protected from the rain and the fierce winds. The birds chirped their thanks, snuggling together for warmth.

"Thank you, Finn. We were too afraid to leave the tree, but you've saved us," one of the birds said gratefully.

Finn didn't stop there. He continued his search for animals in need. He came across a squirrel who had lost his acorns in the storm, a deer whose antlers were caught in a low branch, and even a hedgehog who had rolled himself into a ball in fear of the storm. Finn helped each of them in turn, offering shelter, food, and comfort, doing his best to take care of every animal he met along the way.

As the storm raged on, Finn grew tired, his fur soaked and his paws sore from running so far. But he didn't stop. He knew that the forest was full of creatures that needed his help, and he couldn't rest until everyone was safe.

Finally, as the night wore on, the storm began to subside. The winds calmed, and the rain slowed to a gentle drizzle. The clouds parted, and the moon shone brightly over the forest. Finn made his way back to his cozy den, exhausted but happy. He had helped so many animals, and the forest seemed to have become quieter, calmer, and safer.

As he curled up in his den, he felt a sense of peace in his heart. He didn't need to be the strongest, the fastest, or the smartest animal in the forest. What mattered most was that he cared for others and had done everything he could to help them. His kindness had made a difference, and that was all that mattered.

The next morning, as the sun began to rise, the animals of the forest gathered together in the clearing. They had all emerged from their shelters, and each of them came to find Finn. The rabbits, birds, squirrels, deer, and even the hedgehog all stood together, their eyes shining with gratitude.

"Finn," the rabbit said, stepping forward. "You helped all of us last night. Without you, many of us would have been lost in the storm. You are a true friend, and we are so thankful."

The other animals nodded, and the birds chirped in agreement. Finn smiled, his heart swelling with happiness. "I just did what needed to be done," he said softly. "We all need each other."

The animals of the forest celebrated that day, not just because the storm had passed, but because they had learned an important lesson: kindness was the greatest strength of all. It had brought them together, and it had helped them through the hardest of times.

From that day on, Finn's name was known all over the forest, not just for his kindness, but for the way he taught others that a small act of love could make the world a much better place. And the forest, with its animals and creatures, became a place where kindness and compassion thrived, all because of one little fox who believed in the power of helping others.

5. The Girl Who Could Paint the Stars

In a small village nestled between rolling hills and vast fields, there lived a young girl named Maya. She wasn't like the other children in her village. While they ran and played in the meadows, Maya spent most of her time sitting by the edge of the lake, sketching the world around her. She had always loved art, and her sketches were filled with vibrant colors, swirling patterns, and intricate details. But there was one thing that Maya longed for more than anything else: she wanted to paint the stars.

At night, when the village was quiet and the sky above was a deep shade of blue, Maya would sit outside and gaze up at the stars. She marveled at their brilliance, the way they twinkled and shimmered like diamonds scattered across the dark velvet sky. "If only I could capture that beauty," Maya would whisper to herself.

Maya's family was poor, and she didn't have the finest paints or the best brushes. But she didn't mind. She made do with whatever materials she could find: old brushes, scraps of canvas, and a handful of paints that had been passed down to her by her grandmother. But no matter how hard she tried, she could never quite capture the magic of the stars. Her paintings were lovely, but the stars always seemed out of reach.

One evening, as Maya sat by the lake, a wise old owl named Orion perched on a nearby tree. He had been watching Maya for a long time and had seen her dedication to her craft.

"Why do you look so sad, young one?" Orion asked, his voice gentle but filled with wisdom.

Maya looked up at him, her eyes filled with longing. "I want to paint the stars, but no matter how hard I try, I can never capture their true beauty. They seem too far away, too bright, too perfect for someone like me."

Orion studied Maya for a moment, then nodded his head. "The stars are not meant to be captured, Maya. They are meant to inspire. Sometimes, it is not the exact image that matters, but the feeling they give you—the magic they create in your heart."

Maya thought about Orion's words, but they didn't fully make sense to her. How could she paint the stars if she didn't try to capture their exact image? She spent many more nights painting under the moonlight, always striving to perfect her starry skies.

One evening, as she painted by the lake, a young traveler came through the village. His name was Aiden, and he was an artist just like Maya. He had traveled all over the world, painting the landscapes of every place he visited. When he saw Maya's work, he was immediately struck by the beauty of her paintings, especially the stars.

"You have a gift," Aiden said, smiling warmly. "But I can see that you are frustrated. Why?"

Maya looked at Aiden, unsure of how to explain. "I want to paint the stars perfectly," she said. "I want my paintings to capture their light, their beauty. But no matter what I do, they never look the way I imagine."

Aiden looked at her paintings carefully, studying the way Maya had used color, light, and shadow to express the stars. "Maya," he said gently, "your paintings are not meant to be perfect. You don't need to capture every tiny detail of the stars. What matters is the feeling you create. The stars are already beautiful. What you bring to your painting is the magic of your own heart."

Maya was silent for a moment, her eyes searching the night sky. She had always been focused on making her art perfect, but perhaps Aiden was right. Maybe the magic of the stars wasn't about copying them exactly—it was about expressing the feeling they gave her, the wonder and awe they sparked inside her heart.

That night, Maya tried something different. Instead of focusing on the tiny details of the stars, she let her brush flow freely, letting the colors swirl and mix together as they pleased. She painted the sky with shades of deep blue, lavender, and soft silver, and allowed the stars to dance across the canvas in patterns that felt right to her, not perfect, but full of energy and life.

As she stepped back to admire her work, Maya realized something incredible. Her painting was not like the stars above her, but it was beautiful in its own way. It captured the magic and wonder she felt when she looked up at the sky, and that was enough. The stars didn't need to be perfect; they only needed to inspire.

From that day on, Maya's paintings were filled with the magic of the night sky. She no longer worried about making them perfect. She painted the feelings in her heart, and her art began to speak to others in ways she had never imagined. People from all over came to see her work, and each one saw something different in her paintings—some saw dreams, others saw hope, and some simply saw the beauty of the world around them.

Maya had finally learned that art, like the stars, didn't have to be perfect to be beautiful. It just had to come from the heart.

And so, the girl who wanted to paint the stars discovered something far more precious: she didn't need to capture the stars. She only needed to let the stars inspire her to create something wonderful and unique—a masterpiece of her own.

6. The Courage of Little Leo

In a village surrounded by towering mountains, there lived a small lion cub named Leo. He wasn't the biggest or the fiercest lion in the kingdom, but he had a big heart and a fierce determination. While his friends could roar loudly and run fast, Leo often felt that he wasn't strong enough. He would watch his father, the mighty lion king, lead the pride with authority and confidence, and Leo would wonder if he would ever be able to do the same.

One day, a great danger arrived in the kingdom. A fierce, roaring storm rolled over the mountains, bringing with it terrifying winds and torrential rain. The animals of the kingdom, from the smallest mouse to the tallest giraffe, took shelter in their caves and homes, afraid of the storm's power. The sky was dark, and the wind howled like a wild beast.

The storm raged for days, causing rivers to swell, trees to fall, and the land to be flooded. One evening, as the storm reached its peak, the river near the village began to overflow, and the floodwaters started to rise rapidly. The animals who lived near the river were in danger, and they needed help.

Leo's father, the lion king, knew that he had to act quickly. He gathered the strongest lions of the pride to help save the animals in danger. As Leo watched, he felt a surge of worry and fear. The river was rising fast, and his father was leading the others to help. But Leo was too small. He had never been trained to deal with situations like this, and the thought of facing the rising waters terrified him.

But then he remembered something his father had told him before: "Courage doesn't come from strength alone, Leo. It comes from knowing when to act, even when you're afraid."

Leo's heart raced, but he knew he had to do something. He couldn't just stay hidden in fear while others were in need. Gathering every ounce of courage he could, Leo decided to help, even if it meant stepping out of his comfort zone.

He raced to the riverbank, where the floodwaters were rising quickly. The water was swift and powerful, but Leo didn't hesitate. He remembered the lessons his father had taught him about the importance of helping others, no matter how small the act might seem.

As he approached the river, Leo saw a family of deer trapped on the other side. The water was too deep for them to cross, and they were frightened. Without thinking twice, Leo darted into the rushing water, determined to help.

The current was strong, and the water reached up to his chest, but Leo pressed forward, his legs moving quickly despite the fear gnawing at him. He reached the deer, urging them to follow him. "Come on! Follow me, I'll guide you across!" Leo shouted over the roar of the river.

The deer hesitated, unsure if they could make it across, but Leo didn't give up. With patience and encouragement, he led them one step at a time, helping them move through the dangerous waters. His heart raced, but his determination kept him going.

After what seemed like hours, Leo finally reached the other side of the river, guiding the last of the deer to safety. They were tired, cold, and scared, but they were safe. Leo's legs were shaking, his fur was soaked, but he stood tall with pride.

"You did it, Leo!" one of the deer said, grateful tears in her eyes. "You saved us!"

Leo's heart swelled with happiness. He had faced his fear and helped others, despite feeling small and unsure of himself. But the storm wasn't over. There were still many more animals in danger.

Leo looked back at the river, where the water was still rising. He knew he had to help more. He searched around and saw that his father, the lion king, was struggling to help a group of wild boars caught in the flood. Leo's father, though powerful, was also exhausted from leading the other animals to safety.

Without thinking, Leo ran to his father's side. "Father, let me help," he said, his voice full of determination.

The lion king looked down at his son, surprised to see him so brave. "Leo, you're still young. It's too dangerous."

But Leo didn't back down. "I'm not afraid anymore, Father. I can help. We need to work together."

Seeing the confidence in his son's eyes, the lion king nodded. Together, Leo and his father managed to pull the wild boars to safety, using their combined strength and Leo's quick thinking. They worked side by side, coordinating their efforts, and soon the boars were safely out of the flood's reach.

As the storm finally began to subside, the waters began to recede. The kingdom was saved, and all the animals were safe, thanks to the courage and teamwork of everyone. Leo's father looked at him with pride.

"You were brave, Leo," the lion king said. "You may not be the strongest, but today, you showed me that true courage doesn't come from size or strength—it comes from the heart. You saved lives today, and I couldn't be prouder."

Leo beamed with happiness. He had faced his fear, helped others, and learned an important lesson. He didn't need to be the biggest or the strongest to make a difference—he just needed to be brave and act when others needed him.

From that day forward, Leo no longer doubted himself. He knew that courage wasn't about being fearless; it was about acting in the face of fear, helping others when they needed it most, and believing in himself, even when the task seemed impossible.

And so, Little Leo grew into a lion whose courage was known far and wide, a lion who understood that sometimes, the greatest strength lies in having the courage to do what is right, even when it seems like the odds are against you.

7. The Secret Garden of Hope

In a village nestled at the edge of a vast forest, there lived a young girl named Lily. She was known for her kindness and love for nature, always seen with a basket of flowers or a handful of seeds. However, despite her cheerful appearance, Lily carried a heavy sadness inside her. Her family had once lived in a beautiful house surrounded by colorful gardens, but after a fire destroyed their home, they had to move into a small, humble cottage on the outskirts of the village. Though her new home was cozy, it was surrounded by barren land—gray dirt and broken fences, with no flowers or plants in sight.

Lily missed her old garden terribly. The memories of the vibrant flowers, the sweet scent of roses, and the buzzing of bees were painful reminders of what she had lost. Every day, she would wander outside, wishing she could restore the beauty that had been destroyed. She would stare at the empty land and think, *If only I could make it beautiful again.*

One day, as Lily walked through the village, she saw an old woman sitting by the side of the road. She had a warm smile on her face, but her clothes were old and tattered, and her hair was a silvery gray. Lily felt a sudden pull in her heart and decided to stop.

"Hello, dear," the old woman said kindly. "You seem troubled. What's on your mind?"

Lily hesitated for a moment, then sighed. "I wish I could bring my garden back to life. But the land is so empty and lifeless now. I don't know where to begin."

The old woman nodded thoughtfully. "The land may seem barren, but every garden has the potential to grow, just like every heart. You must first plant the seeds of hope."

Lily was confused. "Seeds of hope?"

The old woman smiled. "Yes, dear. If you believe in something enough and take small steps every day, you will find that what seems impossible can bloom into something beautiful. You have to start with hope, and then nurture it with care and patience."

Lily didn't fully understand the woman's words, but they stuck with her. She thanked the woman and went home, feeling a little lighter than before. That evening, as she sat on her porch, she decided to try something—anything—to make her garden grow again.

The next day, Lily went to the village market and bought some seeds. She chose marigolds, sunflowers, and lavender—flowers she had once loved. Holding the tiny packets in her hands, she went to the empty patch of land behind her house and knelt down. As she dug small holes and planted the seeds, she whispered softly to the earth, "I believe this land can be beautiful again. I believe in the magic of new beginnings."

Each day, Lily cared for her garden with love. She watered the soil, removed the weeds, and made sure the seeds received plenty of sunlight. But despite her best efforts, nothing seemed to happen. The earth remained barren, and Lily began to doubt herself. Maybe the woman's words had been just a dream. Maybe her garden would never come back to life.

One morning, as Lily sat in front of the garden, feeling defeated, she noticed a small sprout poking up from the soil. It was tiny, just a green shoot, but it was there. Lily gasped in surprise and joy. She rushed to water it, feeling her heart swell with hope once again. Over the next few weeks, more sprouts appeared. Little by little, the land that once seemed so lifeless began to change.

As the days passed, the garden started to bloom. The marigolds brightened the earth with their vibrant orange petals, the sunflowers reached for the sky, and the lavender filled the air with its sweet fragrance. Birds and butterflies returned, and the sound of bees buzzing echoed through the garden. It was as if the garden had been waiting all along for someone to believe in it.

One day, as Lily stood in the middle of her beautiful garden, the old woman appeared again, this time with a gentle smile on her face.

"You've done it, dear," the woman said softly. "You planted the seeds of hope, and look at what has bloomed."

Lily smiled, her heart full of gratitude. "Thank you," she said, her voice filled with awe. "I couldn't have done it without your words."

The old woman nodded. "No, dear. You did it yourself. You believed, and you acted. Hope is not just a feeling; it's something we nurture with our actions. The garden didn't grow because of magic, but because you put in the work and believed it could happen. You gave the earth a chance to bloom, and so it did."

Lily looked around at the vibrant garden, a sense of peace filling her. She realized that the garden wasn't just about flowers and plants. It was about hope, resilience, and the power of believing in something better, even when things seem impossible.

From that day on, Lily's garden flourished, and so did her heart. She had learned that even in the darkest times, hope could be planted, nurtured, and grown into something beautiful. And just as the garden bloomed, so too did her belief in herself and the power of new beginnings.

And whenever someone in the village felt lost or sad, Lily would invite them to her secret garden, sharing with them the lesson she had learned: *No matter how barren the land may seem, with hope and love, anything can grow.*

8. The Brave Little Cloud

High above the world, there was a little cloud named Nimbus. He wasn't the biggest or the fluffiest cloud in the sky, but he was curious, full of dreams, and always eager to explore. While the larger clouds drifted lazily across the sky, Nimbus found himself longing to see more of the world below. Every day, he watched as the wind carried the great clouds over mountains, oceans, and forests, leaving beautiful rainbows in their wake. Nimbus wanted to do the same—to bring joy to the earth below and experience the beauty of the world firsthand.

But Nimbus was small, and sometimes, the other clouds would tease him. "You're too tiny to make a difference," they would say, laughing as they passed by. "What could a little cloud like you do?"

At first, these words hurt Nimbus, and he spent many days feeling small and insignificant. But one morning, something wonderful happened. The sun was shining brightly over the land, and the sky was clear, but the weather was growing very hot. Farmers in the fields were worried because their crops were beginning to dry up, and animals in the forest were struggling to find enough water. Nimbus knew this was his chance to do something important.

"I might be small," Nimbus thought, "but I have a purpose. I can help." With this thought, he gathered all the courage he could find and called to the wind. "Please, help me! I want to bring rain to the earth below. I want to help the farmers and animals."

The wind, who had often carried the larger clouds across the sky, heard Nimbus's plea. "Are you sure you're ready for this?" the wind asked. "You're small, but your heart is big. If you truly want to help, you must gather all your strength."

Nimbus nodded eagerly. "I'm ready. I want to try."

With that, the wind swept Nimbus across the sky, carrying him higher and higher. Nimbus felt his tiny body growing heavier as he collected water from the lakes and rivers below. As the wind howled and swirled around him, Nimbus felt the weight of his mission—he had to bring rain, not just for the plants, but for all the creatures in the land who needed it.

At first, Nimbus began to doubt himself. The sky was vast, and there were so many other, bigger clouds who could do the job more easily. Maybe he wasn't strong enough. Maybe he wasn't meant to do this.

But then, he remembered what he had learned: being small didn't mean he couldn't make a difference. It just meant he had to try harder, believe in himself, and use the strength he had.

He focused on gathering more moisture from the air and compacting it together. Slowly but surely, Nimbus began to grow heavier and darker. He felt his tiny body fill with the water that would bring life to the earth. He began to feel proud of his efforts, even though the journey was hard and the wind was fierce.

Finally, after what seemed like an eternity of gathering moisture, Nimbus was full. He had enough water to bring rain to the thirsty land below. With a deep breath, Nimbus summoned all his strength and released the water. The sky grew dark as the first raindrops began to fall. The rain was light at first, but as Nimbus continued to release his moisture, the rain grew heavier and heavier.

The farmers looked up in surprise as the rain began to fall gently on their crops. The animals in the forest cheered as they found puddles to drink from. The earth soaked in the life-giving rain, and everywhere, the plants began to bloom. The heat and dryness that had plagued the land were finally relieved, and everything seemed to come alive again.

Nimbus felt a deep sense of pride as he watched the world below. He had done it. He had brought rain to the earth, and in doing so, he had helped the world grow and thrive. His small size didn't matter anymore. What mattered was the difference he had made by believing in himself and not giving up.

As the storm passed, and the rain slowed to a gentle drizzle, Nimbus felt lighter and freer. The clouds around him, who had once teased him for being small, looked at him with newfound respect. They realized that even though Nimbus wasn't the biggest or the fluffiest cloud, he had done something truly important. They could see the strength and bravery in his heart.

"You did it, Nimbus!" one of the clouds said. "You brought the rain and saved the day. We were wrong to doubt you."

Nimbus smiled, feeling proud but humble. "Thank you," he said, his voice soft but filled with confidence. "I may be small, but I believe that even the smallest of us can make a big difference."

From that day on, Nimbus traveled the sky with a new sense of purpose. He continued to help others, bringing rain when needed and brightening the sky with his presence. And every time he saw a tiny flower bloom or heard the laughter of children playing in the rain, he remembered that being small didn't mean he couldn't change the world.

The brave little cloud had learned that courage, self-belief, and kindness could turn the smallest of dreams into something truly remarkable.

9. The Magic of the Silent Seed

In a peaceful village nestled near the foot of a great mountain, there was a legend that had been passed down for generations. It was said that there was a special seed, known only to the wise elders, that could grow into the most magnificent tree in the world—a tree so magical that its leaves would glow with the colors of the rainbow, and its fruit could heal any ailment.

But there was one important rule: the tree could only be grown by someone who understood the true meaning of patience, kindness, and perseverance. The elders said that no one in the village had yet proven themselves worthy of planting the seed, for the journey to grow such a tree was long and filled with challenges.

Among the children of the village was a young boy named Kai. Kai was curious, always asking questions and seeking adventure. He loved stories about magical trees, and the idea of growing something as extraordinary as the glowing tree fascinated him. He dreamed of one day becoming the person who would be worthy of planting the magical seed.

One evening, as Kai was walking through the village, he overheard a conversation between two of the village elders. They were speaking of the magical seed, and Kai's heart raced with excitement. He gathered the courage to approach them.

"Excuse me," Kai said shyly, "I've heard stories about the magical seed. Is it true? Is it real?"

The elders smiled gently at him. "The seed is real, young one. But it is not for everyone. You see, the seed will only grow for someone who understands that greatness is not achieved by rushing or by force. It grows through silence, patience, and care."

Kai's eyes sparkled. "How can I become worthy? How can I grow the tree?"

The elders exchanged a knowing look. "To grow the tree, you must first understand the power of a silent seed. Only when you have learned to wait, listen, and care for the world around you will you be able to plant the seed and watch it grow."

Kai was determined. He didn't fully understand what the elders meant, but he felt deep in his heart that he was ready to try. They handed him a small pouch containing the precious seed and told him to go to the foot of the mountain, where the soil was rich and fertile. "Go there, and when you are ready, plant the seed. But remember, patience is key."

The next morning, Kai set out on his journey. He walked through forests and crossed streams, climbing higher and higher up the mountain. Along the way, he encountered many challenges: steep cliffs, wild animals, and long, tiring hours of travel. But with each obstacle, Kai remembered the elders' words: patience, silence, care. He took his time, moving carefully, listening to the sounds of the world around him, and respecting the rhythm of nature.

At last, after many days of travel, Kai arrived at a quiet clearing at the base of the mountain. It was a peaceful place, with a clear stream flowing nearby and sunlight filtering through the trees. Kai knew this was the perfect spot for the magical seed.

He knelt down, placed the seed gently into the soft soil, and whispered, "I will take care of you, little seed. I will be patient, and I will wait."

Days turned into weeks, and Kai visited the clearing every day, caring for the spot where he had planted the seed. He watered the soil, protected it from harsh winds, and made sure the area was clean. But there was no sign of the seed sprouting. Kai was starting to lose hope.

One day, after several weeks of waiting, he sat by the seed and sighed. "Maybe the elders were wrong," he thought. "Maybe I'm not meant to grow the magical tree after all."

As he sat in silence, his thoughts began to slow down. He listened to the soft rustle of the leaves in the trees, the gentle flow of the stream, and the chirping of the birds nearby. He realized something important. All this time, he had been so focused on making the seed grow quickly that he had forgotten the true meaning of the journey.

Kai understood now that the magic wasn't just about the tree or the seed—it was about the time spent waiting, the lessons learned, and the care given along the way. The seed, like everything in life, needed time to grow. And so did he.

With a new sense of peace, Kai continued to care for the seed, not out of desperation for it to grow, but because he truly enjoyed the quiet, the stillness, and the beauty of the moment. He learned to live in harmony with nature, appreciating the small things—like the flutter of a butterfly's wings or the way the sunlight danced on the water.

Months passed, and one day, as Kai sat by the seed, something remarkable happened. He felt a small tremor in the earth beneath him. He looked down, and to his amazement, a tiny sprout emerged from the soil. It was small at first, but it was alive.

Kai smiled with joy and pride. His patience had paid off. Over time, the sprout grew into a small sapling, and eventually, it blossomed into a beautiful tree. Its leaves shimmered with the colors of the rainbow, just as the elders had promised, and its fruit radiated a soft, healing glow.

Kai returned to the village with the tree, and the elders greeted him with admiration. "You have done it, Kai," they said. "You understood the magic of the silent seed. You learned that greatness is not rushed—it grows in its own time."

Kai nodded, feeling proud but humble. He knew that the true magic of the tree wasn't just in its beauty or its healing power—it was in the lessons he had learned along the way: patience, perseverance, and the ability to listen to the world around him.

From that day forward, Kai became known as the boy who grew the magical tree, but more importantly, he became a symbol of the power of patience, kindness, and care. And whenever anyone asked him how he did it, he would simply smile and say, "The magic lies not in the seed, but in the quiet moments we take to nurture what is important."

10. The Mountain That Learned to Smile

At the edge of a small village nestled between towering peaks, there was a mountain named Mount Korr. Mount Korr was known far and wide for its great height, its jagged cliffs, and its snow-covered summit. But despite its impressive size, Mount Korr had one very sad problem: it was always grumpy. No one really knew why, but it was said that the mountain was so big and so old that it had forgotten how to smile.

The villagers often spoke of how Mount Korr seemed to frown every time the sun rose, its sharp rocks casting long, cold shadows over the village. When the rain came, the mountain's slopes would seem to groan with displeasure, and when the wind howled, Mount Korr would echo a deep, rumbling sigh. No matter how bright the sky or how warm the sun, Mount Korr always seemed to be grumpy.

The villagers tried many things to cheer up the mountain. They would sing songs, dance around its base, and even offer gifts of flowers and sweet fruits. But nothing worked. Mount Korr remained as grumpy as ever, and the villagers began to believe that the mountain would never be happy.

One day, a young girl named Mira decided she would try to do something no one else had. She had grown up hearing the stories of the mountain's frown and the villagers' failed attempts to make it smile. Mira was different from the others. She was patient and believed that there must be a way to help the mountain.

She climbed the steep path that led up to the foot of Mount Korr, and as she walked, she spoke softly to the mountain. "You don't have to be sad, Mount Korr. I know you've been frowning for a long time, but I think I can help you find your smile."

The mountain, of course, didn't respond. It never had before. But Mira kept walking, step by step, until she reached a large, flat rock where she decided to rest. She sat there quietly, listening to the mountain's winds as they whistled through the trees.

For several days, Mira returned to the same spot, simply sitting and talking to the mountain. She didn't try to force it to smile or change its ways. She simply shared stories with it—stories about the sun rising over the village, about the laughter of children playing, and about the beauty of the stars twinkling in the night sky. At first, the mountain didn't seem to care, but Mira didn't give up.

One day, as Mira was sitting by the mountain's base, something unexpected happened. The clouds parted, and a ray of sunlight broke through the mist, shining directly onto her face. The warmth of the sun made her smile, and without thinking, she whispered, "Even you, Mount Korr, deserve a little sunshine."

Suddenly, the mountain let out a soft, rumbling noise. Mira paused, startled. It wasn't the usual groan, nor the sound of frustration. It was something different, almost like a deep sigh of relief. Mira looked up and gasped. For the first time in her life, she saw the mountain in a new light. The shadows that had always seemed so dark now looked softer, and the jagged cliffs looked less harsh. The mountain seemed to be listening.

Days passed, and Mira continued her quiet visits. She would sit and speak to the mountain, never asking for anything, just sharing her thoughts, her laughter, and her love for the world around her. She would bring small gifts—a bouquet of wildflowers or a song carried by the wind. Slowly but surely, the mountain began to change.

One morning, as Mira arrived, she noticed something magical. The sun was rising, but this time, instead of a dark shadow, the mountain's peak seemed to glow warmly in the early light. There, high above, a soft mist swirled around the top, catching the sunlight in a way that made it sparkle like diamonds. It was as if the mountain was smiling, just a little, for the first time.

Mira sat down, watching in awe. It wasn't the loud, joyful smile she had expected. It was quiet, peaceful, and subtle—like a soft, hidden smile. But it was enough.

From that day on, the mountain's grumpiness began to fade. It was still as large and imposing as ever, but there was a warmth to it now. The villagers noticed that the shadows weren't as harsh, and the winds didn't always carry the same cold sighs. Instead, the mountain seemed to stand a little taller, with a quiet strength that spoke of peace and patience.

Mira continued to visit the mountain, and each time she did, she felt a little more connected to the world around her. She realized that sometimes, just being present, listening, and showing care was enough to bring about change. The mountain had learned to smile, not because someone forced it to, but because someone took the time to understand it and simply be with it.

And so, the legend of Mount Korr changed. No longer was it the grumpy mountain that everyone feared. It became the mountain that smiled in its own quiet way, reminding the villagers that true change comes from patience, understanding, and love.

Mira's simple act of kindness had taught everyone that sometimes, the greatest transformations happen when we stop trying to force change and instead allow it to happen naturally, with care and compassion.

11. The Girl Who Taught the Stars to Dance

In a village that lay beneath the vast, starry sky, there lived a young girl named Amara. She was known for her bright eyes and her ability to see magic in the most ordinary things. Amara's heart was filled with wonder, and she often spent her nights gazing up at the stars, wishing she could understand their secrets. She wondered why the stars twinkled, why they seemed to move in patterns, and why they shone so brightly in the dark sky.

Every night, Amara would sit outside and stare at the constellations, trying to figure out their dance. The stars seemed to tell stories, but she couldn't quite understand their language. She would close her eyes and imagine what it would be like to dance among them, to float in the sky like the moon or the clouds.

One evening, as Amara sat outside, feeling the cool night air, she whispered to the stars, "Oh, how I wish I could dance with you. You're so beautiful, but I don't understand your rhythm. Will you teach me how to dance like you?"

To her surprise, a soft, shimmering voice echoed in the air. It was the voice of the stars.

"Amara, we have watched you for many nights. You are full of wonder, but you have forgotten one important thing. The stars do not simply shine because they are bright. They shine because they are willing to move, to shift, and to change. They dance not with their feet, but with their hearts. If you wish to dance with us, you must first learn to listen to your own heart."

Amara's eyes widened in amazement. "You mean... the stars dance with their hearts?"

The voice of the stars laughed, a soft, melodic sound that seemed to echo through the night air. "Yes, Amara. Every star has its own rhythm, just as every heart does. The stars are not just shining because they are far away; they are shining because they are alive, they are moving, they are filled with light."

Amara thought about this for a long moment. She had always thought the stars were distant and untouchable, but now she realized that they were more than just lights in the sky. They were living beings, full of energy and life, just like her.

"I want to dance with you, stars," she said, her voice full of determination. "Teach me how."

The stars spoke again, this time with more warmth. "Close your eyes, Amara, and listen. Feel the rhythm inside you. Every heartbeat, every breath, is a part of the dance. Let your heart move with the music of the world around you."

Amara took a deep breath and closed her eyes. She tried to listen, to feel the rhythm inside her. At first, it was hard. She couldn't hear anything except the soft rustle of the trees and the whisper of the wind. But then, slowly, something amazing began to happen. She felt a gentle beat inside her chest. It was soft at first, like the distant sound of a drum, but it grew louder and stronger with each breath she took.

She felt her body relax as the rhythm moved through her. It wasn't like dancing to music; it was more like dancing with the very air itself, with the quiet rustling of the leaves, the flicker of the fireflies, and the twinkling of the stars above.

Amara began to sway gently, her arms lifting as if she were floating in the air. The stars seemed to respond to her movements, their light shifting in time with her dance. The constellations above her seemed to swirl and twirl, forming new patterns and shapes, as if the stars themselves were joining her in a graceful dance across the sky.

As Amara danced, she felt her heart expand with joy. She was no longer just a girl staring at the stars. She was a part of the dance, a part of the universe itself. The stars no longer seemed distant or unreachable. They were now her companions, her friends, sharing their light and their rhythm with her.

Hours passed as Amara danced beneath the stars, her movements flowing with the sky above her. The stars shimmered brighter than ever, and the constellations seemed to come alive, their stories unfolding with each movement. For the first time in her life, Amara felt truly connected to the universe.

When she finally stopped and looked up at the sky, she noticed that the stars were no longer just twinkling. They were dancing, just as she had. Their light was softer, more vibrant, and full of warmth. The whole sky seemed to be alive with movement, as if the stars had become part of her dance, and she had become part of theirs.

From that night on, Amara never felt alone when she looked up at the stars. She knew that they were always dancing, always moving with the rhythm of the world. And whenever she felt lost or unsure, she would close her eyes, listen to her heart, and remember the dance she had shared with the stars. She had learned that true beauty and connection come from listening to the rhythm inside and being willing to move with the world around you.

As she grew older, Amara shared her story with others in the village. She taught them that the stars didn't just shine because they were far away—they shone because they were filled with life, movement, and light, just as every heart is. And every night, as she lay down to sleep, Amara would smile, knowing that the stars were still dancing, and that she was part of that magical rhythm.

11. The Girl Who Taught the Stars to Dance

In a village that lay beneath the vast, starry sky, there lived a young girl named Amara. She was known for her bright eyes and her ability to see magic in the most ordinary things. Amara's heart was filled with wonder, and she often spent her nights gazing up at the stars, wishing she could understand their secrets. She wondered why the stars twinkled, why they seemed to move in patterns, and why they shone so brightly in the dark sky.

Every night, Amara would sit outside and stare at the constellations, trying to figure out their dance. The stars seemed to tell stories, but she couldn't quite understand their language. She would close her eyes and imagine what it would be like to dance among them, to float in the sky like the moon or the clouds.

One evening, as Amara sat outside, feeling the cool night air, she whispered to the stars, "Oh, how I wish I could dance with you. You're so beautiful, but I don't understand your rhythm. Will you teach me how to dance like you?"

To her surprise, a soft, shimmering voice echoed in the air. It was the voice of the stars.

"Amara, we have watched you for many nights. You are full of wonder, but you have forgotten one important thing. The stars do not simply shine because they are bright. They shine because they are willing to move, to shift, and to change. They dance not with their feet, but with their hearts. If you wish to dance with us, you must first learn to listen to your own heart."

Amara's eyes widened in amazement. "You mean... the stars dance with their hearts?"

The voice of the stars laughed, a soft, melodic sound that seemed to echo through the night air. "Yes, Amara. Every star has its own rhythm, just as every heart does. The stars are not just shining because they are far away; they are shining because they are alive, they are moving, they are filled with light."

Amara thought about this for a long moment. She had always thought the stars were distant and untouchable, but now she realized that they were more than just lights in the sky. They were living beings, full of energy and life, just like her.

"I want to dance with you, stars," she said, her voice full of determination. "Teach me how."

The stars spoke again, this time with more warmth. "Close your eyes, Amara, and listen. Feel the rhythm inside you. Every heartbeat, every breath, is a part of the dance. Let your heart move with the music of the world around you."

Amara took a deep breath and closed her eyes. She tried to listen, to feel the rhythm inside her. At first, it was hard. She couldn't hear anything except the soft rustle of the trees and the whisper of the wind. But then, slowly, something amazing began to happen. She felt a gentle beat inside her chest. It was soft at first, like the distant sound of a drum, but it grew louder and stronger with each breath she took.

She felt her body relax as the rhythm moved through her. It wasn't like dancing to music; it was more like dancing with the very air itself, with the quiet rustling of the leaves, the flicker of the fireflies, and the twinkling of the stars above.

Amara began to sway gently, her arms lifting as if she were floating in the air. The stars seemed to respond to her movements, their light shifting in time with her dance. The constellations above her seemed to swirl and twirl, forming new patterns and shapes, as if the stars themselves were joining her in a graceful dance across the sky.

As Amara danced, she felt her heart expand with joy. She was no longer just a girl staring at the stars. She was a part of the dance, a part of the universe itself. The stars no longer seemed distant or unreachable. They were now her companions, her friends, sharing their light and their rhythm with her.

Hours passed as Amara danced beneath the stars, her movements flowing with the sky above her. The stars shimmered brighter than ever, and the constellations seemed to come alive, their stories unfolding with each movement. For the first time in her life, Amara felt truly connected to the universe.

When she finally stopped and looked up at the sky, she noticed that the stars were no longer just twinkling. They were dancing, just as she had. Their light was softer, more vibrant, and full of warmth. The whole sky seemed to be alive with movement, as if the stars had become part of her dance, and she had become part of theirs.

From that night on, Amara never felt alone when she looked up at the stars. She knew that they were always dancing, always moving with the rhythm of the world. And whenever she felt lost or unsure, she would close her eyes, listen to her heart, and remember the dance she had shared with the stars. She had learned that true beauty and connection come from listening to the rhythm inside and being willing to move with the world around you.

As she grew older, Amara shared her story with others in the village. She taught them that the stars didn't just shine because they were far away—they shone because they were filled with life, movement, and light, just as every heart is. And every night, as she lay down to sleep, Amara would smile, knowing that the stars were still dancing, and that she was part of that magical rhythm.

13. The Brave Little Cloud

High above the world, where the sky stretched endlessly in all directions, there lived a little cloud named Nimbus. Unlike the other clouds, Nimbus was small, soft, and a little bit shy. The big, puffy clouds would float by in grand formations, casting shadows over the earth below, while Nimbus was often left drifting alone in the corners of the sky.

Nimbus had always admired the larger clouds, who could change shapes into castles, dragons, and ships. They seemed to be so confident and powerful, creating storms and showers whenever they wanted. Nimbus, however, never felt powerful. It was content to float quietly, drifting here and there, watching the world below, but secretly wishing it could do something grand too.

One day, while Nimbus was floating lazily across the sky, it heard the distant sound of crying. It wasn't the usual wind or bird song; it was a soft, sad sound, like the gentle weeping of someone in need. Nimbus looked down and saw a little village nestled between green hills. The villagers were looking up at the sky, worried and afraid. The crops had withered, and the ground was dry and cracked. The rivers had stopped flowing, and the earth seemed to be crying out for rain.

Nimbus felt a tug at its heart. It had never been important before, but now it felt as if it had to do something. It looked over at the large, dark clouds who were floating in the distance, but they didn't seem to care about the village. They were too busy making their own way across the sky, moving without a thought for the needs of the earth below.

With a determined thought, Nimbus floated closer to the village. It knew it wasn't as big or as powerful as the other clouds, but perhaps it could still help.

"I may be small," Nimbus said to itself, "but if I work hard enough, I might be able to make a difference."

Nimbus began to gather the little droplets of water that were floating in the air. It pushed them together, trying to form something bigger. At first, the tiny droplets seemed so scattered, and Nimbus felt like it wasn't making any progress. But it didn't give up. It focused all its energy on gathering more and more moisture, bringing the droplets closer and closer. Slowly, the tiny cloud began to grow. It became a little larger, a little more solid.

As it grew, Nimbus noticed that the villagers were still watching, hoping for rain. Nimbus felt a sense of responsibility. The little cloud had always been afraid of being too small, but now it realized that size didn't matter. It was about what it could do with the strength it had.

Finally, after what felt like hours, Nimbus had gathered enough water to begin its descent. It started to drift over the village, and as it did, it began to release tiny drops of rain. At first, it was just a light drizzle, but then, as Nimbus gathered its courage, the rain grew heavier. The earth soaked up the water, and the villagers began to cheer. The trees perked up, the flowers began to bloom, and the rivers slowly began to fill with water again.

Nimbus felt its heart swell with pride. It may have been small, but it had done something that no one else had thought to do. The village was no longer dry, and the land was beginning to heal. The villagers danced in the rain, grateful for the cloud that had brought the water they so desperately needed.

The larger clouds, who had been watching from afar, now noticed what Nimbus had done. They were amazed. The little cloud, so small and shy, had managed to do something that they, with all their size and power, had overlooked.

Nimbus smiled, feeling a sense of joy and fulfillment that it had never experienced before. It realized that it didn't need to be as big as the other clouds to make a difference. All it needed was to try, to believe in itself, and to act with kindness and determination.

From that day on, Nimbus was no longer the shy, little cloud that drifted alone. It became known throughout the sky as the Brave Little Cloud, the one who had saved the village and brought the rain when it was most needed. And every time Nimbus floated across the sky, it carried with it the knowledge that even the smallest cloud can make a big difference.

14. The Fox Who Found His Voice

In a dense forest surrounded by towering trees and winding rivers, there lived a young fox named Finn. Unlike other foxes, who were known for their sharp wit and clever tricks, Finn had always been quiet. He wasn't shy or afraid; he simply didn't know how to speak the way the others did. While the other animals in the forest communicated through their loud calls and playful chatter, Finn would listen silently from the shadows.

At first, Finn didn't mind being quiet. He liked watching the world around him, enjoying the beauty of the forest without needing to say a word. But over time, he began to feel something was missing. The other animals had friends to talk to, games to play, and stories to share. Finn wanted to join in, but every time he tried to speak, his words never seemed to come out right. He would open his mouth, but only a soft, awkward sound would escape, and the others would look at him with puzzled expressions.

One autumn evening, as Finn sat near a bubbling stream, feeling lonelier than ever, a wise old owl named Orla flew down to a branch beside him.

"Finn," she said in her deep, calm voice, "I've noticed that you've been quiet for some time. You are a clever fox, full of thoughts and ideas. Why do you keep them to yourself?"

Finn looked up at Orla, his eyes full of sadness. "I try to speak, but my words always come out wrong. I don't know how to say what I mean. Everyone else seems to have so much to say, but I'm always silent."

Orla perched on her branch and thought for a moment. "Sometimes, Finn, words are not the only way to communicate. But if you feel the need to speak, you must first listen to your own heart. Find your voice, and it will guide you to speak with meaning."

Finn wasn't sure what Orla meant, but he trusted her wisdom. He decided to spend the next few days in quiet reflection, listening not just to the sounds around him, but to the thoughts inside his own mind. He walked through the forest, watching the animals, listening to the rustling of the leaves, and observing the way the birds called to one another. He tried to pay attention to the things that made him happy, the things that made him sad, and the stories that lived deep inside his heart.

One day, as the sun began to set and the sky was painted in shades of pink and gold, Finn found himself sitting beneath a large oak tree. He closed his eyes, took a deep breath, and felt a strange warmth growing inside him. It wasn't just the warmth of the setting sun; it was something inside him, a feeling that he couldn't quite explain.

Suddenly, a thought appeared in his mind. He had something he wanted to say. It wasn't complicated or clever, just a simple truth that had been waiting to be spoken.

"I'm here," he whispered softly, almost to himself.

And to his surprise, his words didn't feel awkward at all. They felt right. Finn felt a rush of relief. It was as if the words had finally found their place, and they had been waiting for the right moment to come out.

The next day, Finn decided to share his new-found voice. He walked up to a group of squirrels playing near the stream. The squirrels, who were busy chattering and scampering about, paused when they saw him.

"Hello," Finn said, his voice clear and strong, though still a little soft.

The squirrels looked at each other in surprise. They had never heard Finn speak before, but there was something about his voice that made them listen. Finn took a deep breath and added, "I've been thinking... I may not have many words, but I have stories to share."

The squirrels, intrigued by Finn's sincerity, nodded and gathered around him. Finn began to tell them stories about his adventures in the forest, the things he had seen, and the animals he had met. He didn't need to speak loudly or quickly; his words came gently, like the breeze through the trees. And to his delight, the squirrels listened intently, laughing at his tales and asking him questions.

From that moment on, Finn discovered that he didn't have to speak like everyone else. He didn't need to shout or be the loudest; he just needed to speak from his heart, and when he did, others would listen.

As the days passed, Finn found more and more animals willing to listen to his stories. The birds, the deer, and even the rabbits came to him with questions and stories of their own. Finn no longer felt alone. He realized that his voice was special, just as he was, and that sometimes, the most meaningful words were the ones that came from the heart, not the loudest or the most clever.

Finn's voice may have been soft, but it carried wisdom, kindness, and a gentle strength. He learned that everyone has something valuable to share, and that silence doesn't mean you have nothing to offer. Sometimes, it takes patience and understanding to find your voice, but when you do, the world will listen.

And so, Finn the fox became known throughout the forest as the storyteller who spoke with his heart. He had found his voice, not in the noise of the world, but in the quiet moments where he listened to his own thoughts, and that made all the difference.

15. The Brave Little Seed

In a quiet corner of a vast forest, nestled deep within the earth, a small seed lay beneath the soil. This seed, unlike the others, was unsure about the world above. It had heard stories from the older seeds about the sun's warmth, the breeze's gentle touch, and the beautiful flowers that bloomed from seeds like them. But the little seed wasn't sure if it was ready to face the world. It felt small, scared, and uncertain.

"I don't know if I can do it," the little seed whispered to itself. "What if I'm not strong enough to grow? What if I'm not like the other seeds?"

But as time passed, the little seed couldn't help but listen to the sounds of the forest above. The birds sang, the animals moved through the trees, and the wind rustled the leaves. The forest seemed alive, vibrant, and full of potential. The little seed felt a pull, a quiet desire to be a part of it all, but still, it doubted its own strength.

One day, as the rain began to fall, the seed felt a gentle nudge from the soil. The earth was moist, the air was fresh, and something deep inside the seed stirred. "Maybe today is the day," it thought. "Maybe today, I will finally begin my journey."

With courage that it didn't know it had, the little seed began to push upward, breaking through the soil. At first, the journey was slow. The soil was thick, and the weight of the earth above it was heavy. The little seed felt its tiny roots stretching, reaching for the life-giving water beneath the surface. It was hard, and the seed thought about giving up, but it pressed on, step by step.

Finally, after what felt like an eternity, the seed felt a gentle warmth on its surface. It had reached the top of the soil and was greeted by the sunlight for the very first time. The warmth felt comforting, like a soft hug from the sky.

The little seed was no longer afraid. It stood tall, reaching for the sun, and in time, it began to grow into a small plant. Its leaves unfurled, soaking in the light and the warmth, and slowly, it grew stronger with each passing day.

As the days turned into weeks, the plant blossomed into a beautiful flower. It had bright petals that shimmered in the sunlight, and its fragrance filled the air. The little seed that had once been so unsure of itself had become a vibrant part of the forest, and it realized that the journey of growth was not about being perfect or strong from the start. It was about believing in itself, pushing through the challenges, and trusting that with time, it would bloom into something beautiful.

The little flower stood proudly in the forest, surrounded by other plants and creatures, knowing that it had the strength to face whatever came next. It had found its place in the world, and it was no longer afraid to grow.

16. The Dolphin Who Couldn't Jump

In a vast, sparkling ocean, there lived a young dolphin named Kai. Kai was a playful and joyful dolphin, always swimming alongside his pod, leaping and darting through the waves. But there was one thing that Kai couldn't do, and it made him feel different from the other dolphins.

Kai couldn't jump.

Every time the pod would gather together for their daily play, the other dolphins would leap high into the air, twisting and spinning before splashing back into the water with a joyful splash. It was a beautiful sight to see, and everyone cheered for the dolphins who performed the most graceful, daring jumps. But no matter how hard Kai tried, he just couldn't leap the way the others could. His jumps were small and clumsy, and sometimes he would land with a soft splash that barely caused a ripple.

Kai felt frustrated. He loved swimming, and he wanted to be just as graceful as the others. He wanted to make his pod proud, but no matter how much he practiced, his jumps were never as high or as beautiful. One day, as the dolphins played, Kai swam to the edge of the group, feeling defeated.

"Why can't I jump like the others?" he wondered aloud, his voice heavy with disappointment.

Just then, a wise old sea turtle named Tavi, who had been watching the young dolphins for some time, slowly paddled over to Kai.

"Kai," Tavi said gently, "why are you so sad?"

Kai looked up at the wise turtle, his eyes full of frustration. "I want to jump like the others, but no matter how hard I try, I can't. I'm just not good at it. Maybe I'm not meant to be a great dolphin like them."

Tavi nodded thoughtfully. "Sometimes, we get so caught up in what we think we should be that we forget who we truly are. Not every dolphin is meant to jump the same way. But that doesn't mean you don't have something special."

Kai looked at Tavi, confused. "But I don't jump like them. I can't even do a flip in the air like the others."

Tavi smiled slowly, his wise eyes gleaming. "Kai, you may not jump the way the others do, but you have something that they do not. You have the ability to dive deeper than any dolphin I've ever seen. When you swim, you move through the water with such grace and strength that the ocean itself seems to open up just for you. You don't need to jump to be special. You need to embrace who you are and the gifts you have."

Kai thought about Tavi's words, and for the first time, he truly noticed the way he swam. He loved the deep dives he took, feeling the water rushing past him, the currents guiding him like a gentle current. He could swim so deep that the world above seemed to disappear, and he could explore hidden caves and coral reefs with ease.

The next day, when the dolphins began their jumping play, Kai decided to do something different. Instead of trying to jump, he dove deep into the ocean, feeling the coolness of the water wrap around him like a blanket. He swam with the currents, exploring the hidden treasures of the ocean floor.

As Kai swam gracefully beneath the water, the other dolphins began to notice. They watched in awe as Kai moved through the deep water, his sleek body gliding effortlessly. They had never seen a dolphin swim quite like him before. Kai wasn't just good at swimming; he was exceptional.

From that day on, Kai embraced his unique skill. He no longer felt the need to jump in the same way the others did. He had found his own path, one that was just as special and valuable. The other dolphins began to admire Kai's diving skills and would often ask him to lead them on deep-water explorations. Kai had found his place in the pod, and he realized that it was okay to be different. He didn't need to compare himself to others; he simply needed to embrace who he was and celebrate the gifts he had.

17. The Star That Was Afraid to Shine

In a distant galaxy, among countless twinkling stars, there was one star named Luma who was afraid to shine. Luma had always been smaller than the other stars, with a soft glow that barely flickered in the dark sky. Every night, when the stars lit up the sky in their brilliant patterns, Luma would hide in the corner, afraid that its dim light would make it stand out in a bad way. It wasn't like the other stars, who shone brightly, casting their light across the universe.

"I don't want to be seen," Luma thought, hiding behind the larger, more radiant stars. "What if my light is too small? What if it doesn't matter?"

But one evening, as the moon cast a gentle glow over the Earth below, a little girl named Emma looked up at the night sky. She was lying on the soft grass in her backyard, watching the stars twinkle above her. Emma had always loved stargazing. To her, the stars were magical, each one holding a special wish, a secret, or a story.

"Look, Mommy!" Emma pointed to the sky. "That star is so beautiful. It's shining just for me."

Her mother smiled, following Emma's gaze. "Yes, my dear, every star has its own light. Some are big, and some are small, but they all shine for someone, somewhere."

Emma's words reached Luma's ears, and for the first time, Luma felt something stir deep within. It wasn't about being the brightest star, it was about shining for someone who needed it. Luma realized that even though it was small, its light could make a difference to someone, just like the way Emma noticed it from below.

That night, for the first time, Luma decided to shine without fear. It focused on its own light, letting its soft glow spread across the sky. At first, it was just a tiny flicker, but slowly, it grew stronger, brighter. The longer it shone, the more Luma realized that the sky was vast and filled with other stars, each one contributing its own special glow.

As the days passed, Luma learned that being afraid to shine had kept it from sharing its true self with the world. Every night, as it sparkled in the sky, it remembered Emma's smile and her belief in the beauty of the stars. Luma realized that even though it was small, it mattered. It didn't need to compete with the other stars—it just needed to be itself.

From that night on, Luma shone brighter and brighter, not for anyone else, but for itself. It understood that its light had a place in the universe, and that it was beautiful just the way it was. The stars no longer seemed so intimidating. Luma had found its own confidence, and it began to shine boldly, knowing that every star had a unique purpose.

18. The Little Lion Who Learned to Roar

In the heart of the great savanna, there lived a young lion named Leo. Leo was strong and fast, with a golden mane that shimmered in the sun. But there was one thing Leo couldn't do—he couldn't roar.

All the other lions in the pride could roar loudly and fearlessly. Their roars echoed across the savanna, warning other animals of their presence and showing their dominance. Leo, however, could only manage a small, squeaky sound. Every time he tried to roar, nothing came out, or his roar was too soft to be heard.

Leo was embarrassed. He wanted to roar like the other lions, to feel the power in his voice, to show everyone that he was brave and strong. He would practice every day, standing tall and trying to summon his roar, but it never came out the way he wanted.

One evening, after watching the older lions roar proudly at the setting sun, Leo walked to a quiet spot in the savanna, feeling discouraged. "I'm not like the others," he thought sadly. "I can't roar. I'll never be a true lion."

Just then, a wise old tortoise named Tamu slowly approached Leo. Tamu had lived in the savanna for many years, and he had seen many animals grow and change. He saw the sadness in Leo's eyes and knew exactly what the young lion needed.

"Leo," Tamu said kindly, "why are you so sad?"

"I can't roar," Leo replied, his voice low. "I want to be like the others. I want to show them that I'm strong and brave. But no matter how hard I try, my roar is just too soft."

Tamu chuckled softly and sat down beside Leo. "You're looking at roars the wrong way, young one. Roaring doesn't always show strength. It's not about how loud or strong your voice is, it's about the courage behind it."

Leo looked at Tamu, puzzled. "What do you mean?"

Tamu smiled wisely. "Roaring is a way of showing who you are and claiming your place in the world. But it's not the roar that defines you, it's your actions. You don't need to be the loudest lion. Your heart and your strength come from within, not from the noise you make."

Leo thought about Tamu's words for a long time. The next day, when the pride gathered again, Leo decided to try something different. Instead of focusing on making a loud roar, he stood tall and spoke from his heart. He let his voice be gentle, but full of confidence. "I may not roar like the others," Leo said, "but I am a lion, strong and proud in my own way."

To his surprise, the other lions stopped and listened. They weren't focused on the volume of Leo's voice, but on the courage and wisdom behind it. Leo realized that it wasn't the loudness that mattered; it was the belief in himself and the strength he carried inside.

From that day on, Leo no longer felt the need to compare himself to the others. He understood that each lion had its own unique way of showing strength. And even though his roar was soft, it came from a place of true bravery. Leo was a lion, proud of who he was, and his roar—gentle but powerful—was enough.

19. The Elephant Who Couldn't Forget

In a lush, green jungle, there lived a young elephant named Kavi. Kavi was known for his keen memory—he could remember every tree, every river, and every path he had ever taken. He could recall the smallest details from his days as a calf, and he could remember the faces of every animal in the jungle.

But there was one thing Kavi could never forget, and it troubled him deeply. He had made a mistake when he was younger. One day, while playing with the other young animals, Kavi had accidentally knocked over a tree, damaging the homes of several smaller creatures. Though it was an accident, Kavi never stopped blaming himself. Every time he walked through the jungle, he would see the tree and feel a pang of guilt in his heart.

"I should have been more careful," Kavi thought sadly. "I hurt others, and no matter how hard I try, I can't seem to forget what I've done."

The other animals in the jungle had long forgiven Kavi, but he couldn't forgive himself. His memories weighed heavily on him, and he couldn't seem to move forward.

One day, while wandering near the river, Kavi met an old, wise crocodile named Tula, who had lived in the jungle for many years. She had seen countless animals come and go, and she knew much about life and its challenges.

"Kavi," Tula said, "I can see that something is bothering you. What weighs on your heart?"

Kavi sighed deeply. "I can't stop thinking about the mistake I made when I was younger. I know it was an accident, but I can't forget it. I hurt others, and I don't think I can ever move on."

Tula looked at Kavi with understanding. "Ah, young one, the past has a way of clinging to us. But holding on to guilt will only keep you stuck in one place. The jungle is full of second chances. You must learn to forgive yourself, just as the others have forgiven you."

"But how?" Kavi asked. "How can I let go of something that I can never undo?"

Tula smiled gently. "You must remember that every living thing in this jungle makes mistakes. You, too, are part of this ever-changing cycle of life. What matters is not the mistake itself, but what you do with it. Have you tried to make amends for what happened?"

Kavi nodded. "I've tried. I've helped rebuild homes, and I've apologized to everyone who was affected. But still, the memory lingers."

Tula slowly swam closer to Kavi, her eyes filled with wisdom. "Let me tell you something. The trees, the rivers, and the animals all grow and change. They don't dwell on the past but continue to live, grow, and flourish. The mistake you made doesn't define you. It is what you choose to do now that matters."

Kavi thought about Tula's words for a long time. He realized that even though the past could not be changed, he had the power to move forward and make a positive difference in the present. Slowly, he began to forgive himself, letting go of the weight that had been holding him back.

Over time, Kavi learned that it was okay to make mistakes, as long as he learned from them and worked to make things better. He no longer let the past haunt him. Instead, he used his memory and his kindness to help others in the jungle, knowing that every day was a new opportunity to grow.

20. The Butterfly Who Couldn't Fly

In a beautiful garden full of vibrant flowers, there lived a young caterpillar named Lyra. Lyra was different from the other caterpillars. While they were content to crawl along the branches and leaves, Lyra dreamed of flying. She would look up at the butterflies fluttering through the sky, their wings colorful and graceful, and wish that one day she could be just like them.

"One day," she would say to herself, "I will be able to fly too."

But as Lyra crawled along the leaves, she couldn't help but notice how different she was. She had small legs, a soft body, and no wings. The other caterpillars would tell her, "One day, you'll change. You'll grow wings and fly." But Lyra wasn't so sure. She didn't feel ready for change, and the idea of transforming into something so different from what she was felt scary.

One day, a wise old butterfly named Mira fluttered down to Lyra. Mira was older and had seen many caterpillars like Lyra go through their transformations.

"Why do you look so worried, little one?" Mira asked with a gentle smile.

"I'm afraid," Lyra admitted. "I don't know if I can ever be like the other butterflies. What if I can't fly when I change? What if I'm not ready?"

Mira chuckled softly. "Change can be scary, but it is also a part of life. Every butterfly, every caterpillar, must go through a process before they can fly. The most important thing is to trust the change that's happening inside of you."

"But how can I trust something I can't see?" Lyra asked.

Mira's wings fluttered gently in the breeze. "You don't need to see it. You only need to trust in the process. You are already becoming something beautiful, even if you can't see it yet. All you have to do is be patient and trust yourself."

Lyra wasn't completely sure, but she decided to follow Mira's advice. She continued to crawl along the leaves, eating and resting, all the while feeling the strange changes happening inside her body. Days passed, and one morning, she felt something new—she was no longer a caterpillar. Her body had transformed into a cocoon.

Inside the cocoon, Lyra was both scared and excited. She didn't know what was happening to her, but she remembered Mira's words. "Trust yourself."

Finally, after what felt like an eternity, Lyra felt a powerful urge to break free. Slowly, she emerged from her cocoon, and to her amazement, she had beautiful, colorful wings! Her wings shimmered in the sunlight, and she could feel the breeze beneath her. She spread them wide, took a deep breath, and fluttered into the air.

Lyra was flying!

The fear she had felt melted away as she soared through the sky, the wind lifting her higher and higher. She realized that even though the transformation had been difficult and uncertain, it had led her to become exactly what she had always dreamed of—a butterfly. Lyra understood now that sometimes, the scariest changes lead to the most beautiful results.

From that day on, Lyra flew freely through the garden, knowing that no matter how hard or scary change might seem, it was always worth it in the end.